W9-BRB-081

CHINA

Janet Riehecky

Lerner Publications Company • Minneapolis

The editor wishes to thank Wang Ping for her careful review of this book.

Lerner Publications Company
A division of Lerner Publishing Group, Inc.
241 First Avenue North
Minneapolis, MN 55401 U.S.A.

Website address: www.lernerbooks.com

Library of Congress Cataloging-in-Publication Data

Riehecky, Janet, 1953–
        China / by Janet Riehecky.
            p.   cm. — (Country explorers)
        Includes index.
        ISBN: 978–0–8225–7129–2 (lib. bdg. : alk. paper)
        1. China—Juvenile literature. I. Title.
    DS706.R54 2008
        915.1—dc22   2006036731

Manufactured in the United States of America
1 2 3 4 5 6 – JR – 13 12 11 10 09 08

Table of Contents

Welcome!

We're traveling to China! China is one of the world's largest countries. It lies on the world's biggest continent—Asia. Beijing is China's capital.

The Pacific Ocean meets China's east coast. Thick forests and more of the Pacific Ocean lie to the south. High mountains and dry deserts separate China from countries to the north and west.

Beijing is in northern China. About 15 million people call the city home.

RUSSIA

KAZAKHSTAN

Urümqi

KYRGYZSTAN

TARIM BASIN

TAJIKISTAN

TAKLIMAKAN DESERT

AFGHANISTAN   PAKISTAN

PLATEAU OF TIBET

TIBET

NEPAL

Mount Everest

INDIA

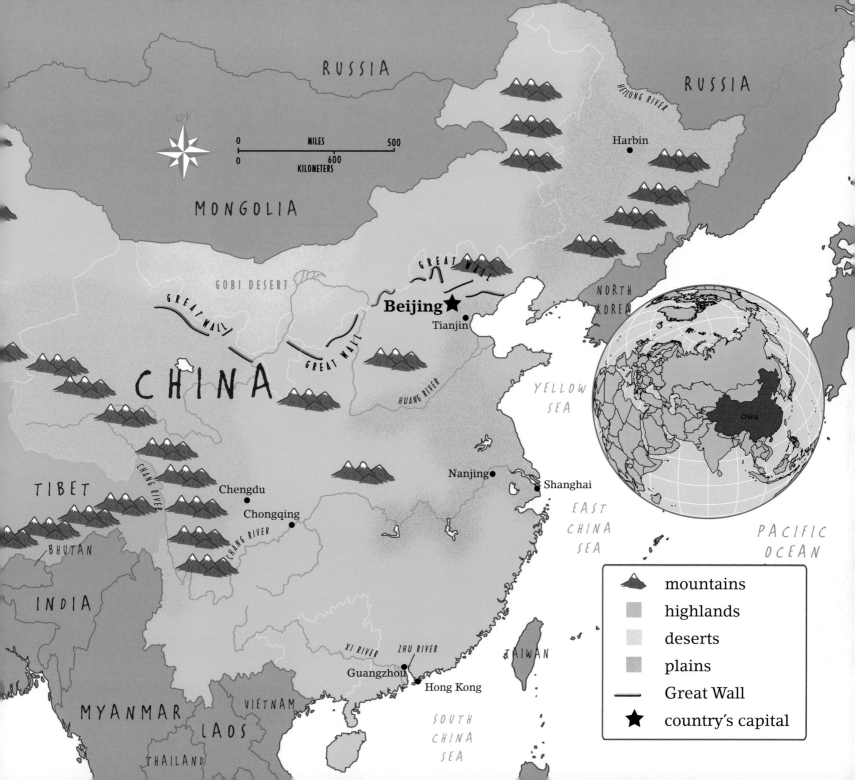

Step Up!

China is like a giant staircase. The bottom step sits in the east. This part of China has farmland and rivers.

The middle of China is the second step. This step has mountains, basins, and plateaus.

Rice is a common crop on China's farms.

6

Western China is the top step. High mountains and cold plateaus lie there. The landscape makes it a tough place to live.

Map Whiz Quiz

Take a look at the map on pages 4 and 5. A map is a drawing or chart of a place. Trace the outline of China onto a sheet of paper. See if you can find the East China Sea. Mark this part of your map with an *E* for *east*. How about the country of Mongolia? Mark this with an *N* for *north*. Find the Huang River and the Chang River. Trace these rivers with the color blue. Next find the Great Wall of China. Color it red.

The Himalayas are a rugged mountain range in southwestern China.

7

Seas and Rivers

Seas touch some of China's shores. The Yellow Sea is in the northeast. The East China Sea is in the east. To the south lies the South China Sea.

Thousands of rivers run through China. The Chang River is the third-longest river in the world. The Huang River is sometimes called the Yellow River because of its color. Yellow soil turns the river's water yellow!

China's main rivers flow to the east, where the Pacific Ocean lies.

8

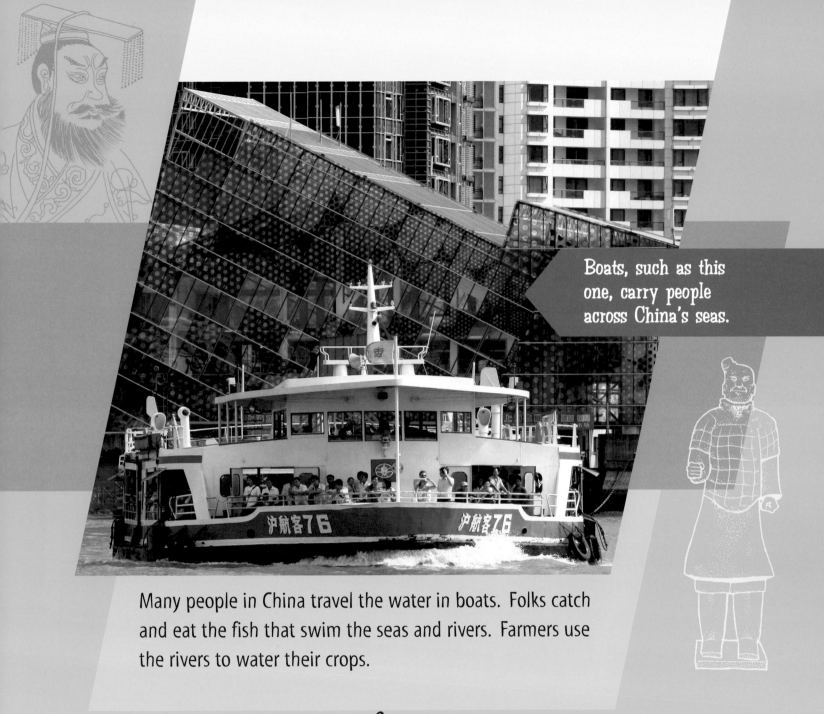

Boats, such as this one, carry people across China's seas.

Many people in China travel the water in boats. Folks catch and eat the fish that swim the seas and rivers. Farmers use the rivers to water their crops.

Chinese People

China has the biggest population of any country in the world. More than one billion people live there. Most Chinese people are called Han. The Han share traditions and a rich culture. They speak a language called Mandarin Chinese.

China's city streets are crowded!

Some Chinese people aren't Han. They speak different languages. They have their own traditions too.

The Miao people live in China. These Miao girls are wearing traditional clothing.

Three Is a Family

Many kids in China have no brothers or sisters. They might live with just their moms and dads. There are so many people in China that the government made a rule. The rule said that families should have only one child.

One-child families are common in China.

But not all Chinese families have only one child. Some families in the country are allowed to have two children. And Chinese families are not always small. Grandparents, aunts, uncles, and cousins make families big. Relatives often live near one another. They might often have get-togethers.

This Chinese family is enjoying a meal together.

Family Words

Here are the Chinese words for family members.

grandfather	zufu	(dzoo-foo)
grandmother	zumu	(dzoo-moo)
father	fuqin	(foo-chihn)
mother	muqin	(moo-chihn)
uncle	shushu	(shoo-shoo)
aunt	ayi	(ah-ee)
son	er.zi	(ER-dzeh)
daughter	nuer	(noo-er)
older brother	ge.ge	(GUH-guh)
younger brother	de.de	(DEE-dee)
older sister	jie.jie	(JEE-EH-jee-eh)
younger sister	mei.mei	(MAY-may)

In the City

Beep! Beep! Chinese cities are noisy places. Millions of people live in Beijing, Shanghai, and Tianjin. The roads are jammed with people walking, biking, and driving.

This bustling street is in Hong Kong.

14

Some city folks have houses. But many people live in apartments. There are not enough apartments to go around. Two families might share one apartment.

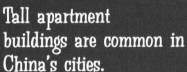

Tall apartment buildings are common in China's cities.

On the Farm

Many Chinese people live on farms. Some farmers grow rice in wet fields called paddies. Others raise wheat and soybeans.

Farmers work hard in China's rice paddies.

Markets in China are often outdoors. This family drove their motorbike to the market!

Farmers sell some of the food to the government. The rest goes to colorful markets.

Getting Around

People in China get around in many different ways. They drive cars. They ride buses. They also take subways and trains. China's city streets are often crowded.

Trams such as this provide an easy way to get from place to place in China.

18

These bikers in Shanghai share the road with lots of traffic!

Many Chinese people ride bikes from place to place. But biking in the city can be hard. Bikers must share the streets with cars, buses, and taxi cabs.

19

Long Ago in China

Emperors ruled China for four thousand years. The emperors were rich. But most people were poor. In 1911, the Chinese decided not to let emperors rule anymore.

The Great Wall of China is very famous. An emperor started building the wall more than two thousand years ago.

In 1949, a new group took over. They were called the
Communist Party. China became known as the People's
Republic of China. People called it the PRC for short.

Dear Uncle Stan,

Today I visited the Forbidden City in
Beijing. Long ago, it was the emperor's
palace. These days, it is a museum. I
saw a gold throne the emperor sat in!
Later, I was hungry, so Mom let me buy
a roll filled with meat. A girl my age
sold it to me from a cart on the
street! It was yummy.

Love,
Emmeline

Unc
Anyw

Forbidden City, Beijing

故宫博物院

21

Speaking Chinese

In China, it's not just what you say. It is also how you say it. The Chinese language has four tones. Chinese speakers can change a word's meaning simply by changing the tone of their voice. Here is an example. The word *ma* can mean "mother" or "horse." No kidding!

Schoolchildren laugh and talk with one another. Do you think they're speaking Chinese?

China's schools teach students to speak one form of the Chinese language.

People in different parts of China speak Chinese in different ways. In schools across China, kids learn to speak the same kind of Chinese. That way, people all over the country can use the same language to talk to one another.

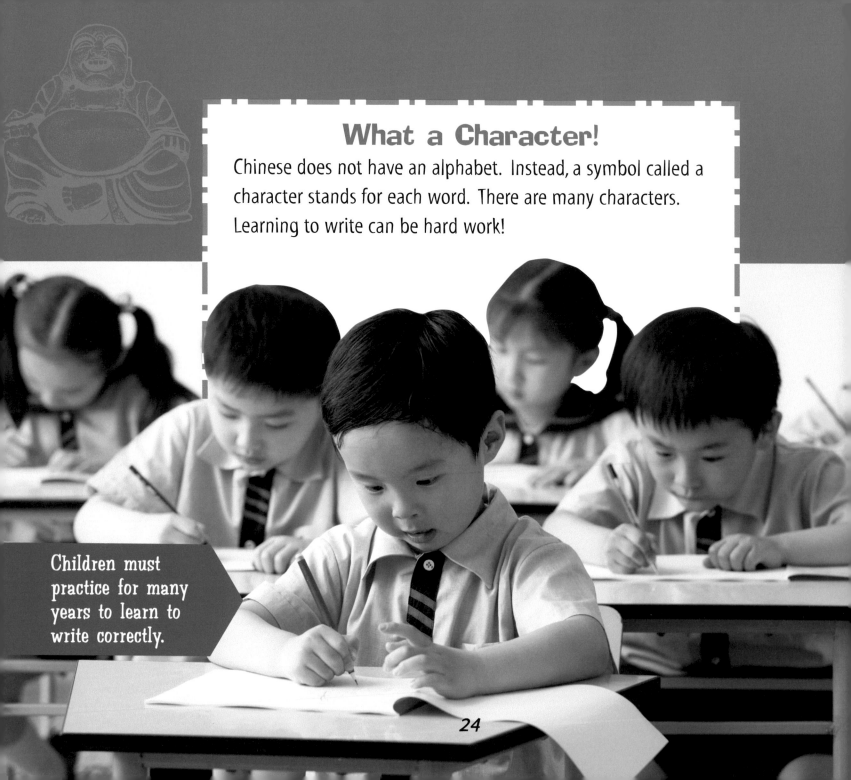

What a Character!

Chinese does not have an alphabet. Instead, a symbol called a character stands for each word. There are many characters. Learning to write can be hard work!

Children must practice for many years to learn to write correctly.

Drawing characters is a form of art in China. Writers use special brushes and black ink. They copy the characters onto white sheets of paper.

This Chinese character means "love."

Faith and Respect

Children in China respect older people. The Chinese believe that older people are wise. Young people ask their grandparents for advice when times are confusing.

Chinese grandparents share their knowledge with younger family members.

The Biggest Buddha

Some people in China believe in the Buddha's teachings. The Buddha was a religious leader. He lived long ago. The world's biggest statue of the Buddha is carved in the side of a cliff in China. It took workers about one hundred years to carve. Two people can sit side by side on one of the statue's toenails!

Often the older person has a helpful answer. Chinese people also believe in sharing and cooperation.

Cooperation is an important value in China. Schoolchildren learn to work and play together.

Happy New Year!

Chinese New Year is a special holiday. Everyone wants the new year to have a happy start. A huge party takes place. The party lasts for fifteen days.

Children get red envelopes on Chinese New Year. The envelopes have gifts of money inside.

Parades fill the streets. People make giant puppets dance. A lion puppet at the beginning of the parade scares away bad spirits. A long paper dragon puppet ends the parade.

Water Dragon

Why does a dragon puppet end the parade? In Chinese stories, dragons are not scary. They are wise and helpful. They bring people water to help crops grow. So in China, a dragon puppet brings good luck at the end of a parade.

A dragon lantern brightens a Chinese New Year celebration.

School Days

Reading, writing, and arithmetic—that's what Chinese students study. Does that sound like what you learn about in school?

Chinese students study many of the same subjects you do!

These students are from Shanghai.

Kids in China go to elementary school, just like kids in the United States. Many Chinese teenagers stay in school and go on to college. But some take jobs instead.

南屏山 昇月 曹操

Story Time
The Chinese tell many stories. Some are about adventures. Others are long poems or folktales. Some stories are new. Others are very old.

This picture shows a scene from *The Romance of the Three Kingdoms*, a famous Chinese story.

32

Folktales that teach lessons are popular. These stories might be about sharing. They might be about helping others.

A young boy in traditional clothing reads about Chinese culture. Folktales are an important part of China's culture.

"The Magic Goldfish"

Once upon a time, there lived a young woman named Ye Shen. Ye Shen had a wicked stepmother. The stepmother killed Ye Shen's pet goldfish. Ye Shen was sad. She kept the fish's bones to remind her of her pet.

One day, everyone in town went to a festival. Ye Shen had to stay home. She had no nice clothes to wear. But then something amazing happened. The fish bones saved the day! They turned out to be magical. They gave Ye Shen beautiful clothes. Ye Shen went to the festival. At the party, a king fell in love with her. But Ye Shen left before the king learned her name. She also left something behind—her shoe! Can you guess how the story ends? Hint: Think of *Cinderella*.

Clothes

People in China wear all different kinds of clothes. Lots of people choose comfortable shirts or pants. Their clothes might look a lot like the clothes you wear.

Comfortable clothes are a popular choice in China.

34

Some city folks wear suits and ties or dresses. Others love the latest fashions.

Silk

The Chinese invented silk. Silk is a smooth, shiny fabric. It comes from silkworms. Silkworms are a kind of caterpillar. People make silk from the cocoons of silkworms. Skilled workers unwind the cocoons. Then they weave silk from the strands of the cocoons.

These people in Hong Kong are dressed to go to work.

Playtime

Martial arts are popular in China. Martial arts are a type of exercise. They are also a form of self-defense. Some people practice martial arts each morning. They meet in parks and exercise together.

Young martial arts students giggle during class.

People fly all kinds of kites at a special festival in the city of Weifang.

Kids in China love to fly kites. Table tennis is popular too. Gymnastics is a favorite sport. Many Chinese gymnasts have gone to the Olympics.

Doctors

Can sticking your skin with a needle cure a headache? A Chinese doctor might think so! This practice is called acupuncture. The Chinese believe acupuncture can cure more than one hundred diseases. But do not try this at home! Only experts know how to do acupuncture correctly.

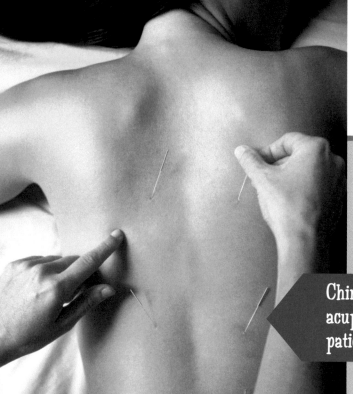

Chinese doctors use acupuncture to help patients feel better.

Acupuncture is a traditional cure in China. Not all Chinese doctors use acupuncture. Many give out pills and use modern tools instead. Some doctors use both modern and traditional methods.

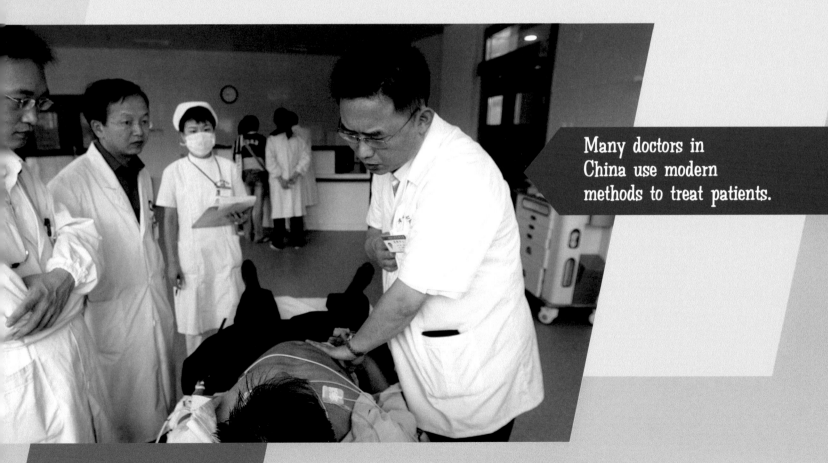

Many doctors in China use modern methods to treat patients.

Fruit is for sale at this outdoor market.

Shopping for Food

Many Chinese people shop at outdoor markets. There they buy fresh foods to eat. They might spend lots of time looking for the best prices.

40

People in China eat many different foods. In the south, farmers grow a lot of rice. People who live nearby eat rice at almost every meal. In the north, wheat is a major crop. People there make wheat into noodles. Cooked vegetables are important parts of meals across China.

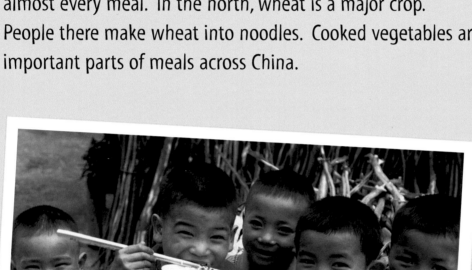

Noodles and rice are important parts of people's diets in China.

Mealtime!

Yummy stir-fries are popular in China. First, a cook chops meat and veggies into bite-size pieces. The next step is frying the food over a hot fire.

A chef prepares a meal outdoors in Beijing.

42

Stir-fried veggies are crunchy and delicious!

If you ate a meal in China, you may not use a fork or spoon. Instead, you might use chopsticks! Chopsticks are long, thin sticks. People hold them in one hand. Experts use them like a pair of fingers. It takes a long time to learn to use chopsticks well.

The cook stirs the food in a pan called a wok. Stirring keeps the food from burning while it fries.

THE FLAG OF CHINA

China's flag is red and yellow. Five yellow stars sit in the upper left-hand corner of the solid red flag. Red is an important color in China. The Chinese people often use red in festivals. Red also stands for the Communist Party. People have different ideas about what the yellow stars stand for. Some say they stand for the People's Republic of China. Others say they stand for China's ethnic groups. Still others think the stars stand for unity. China's citizens are unified in the People's Republic of China.

FAST FACTS

FULL COUNTRY NAME: People's Republic of China

AREA: 3.7 million square miles (9.6 million square kilometers), or about the same size as the United States

MAIN LANDFORMS: the mountain ranges the Himalayas, Kunlun, Pamirs, and Tian Shan; the deserts Gobi, Mu Us, and Taklimakan; the plateau called Plateau of Tibet

MAJOR RIVERS: Huang, Chang, Xi, Heilong, Li

ANIMALS AND THEIR HABITATS: Bactrian camels (desert), Chinese alligators (river, stream, lake, pond, and swamp), Chinese river dolphins (river), giant pandas (forest)

CAPITAL CITY: Beijing

OFFICIAL LANGUAGE: Mandarin Chinese

POPULATION: about 1,313,973,713

GLOSSARY

basin: a hollow place in the land, often with a lake at the bottom. Basins are near mountain ranges.

capital: a city where the government is located

character: a picture or symbol that stands for a whole word or for a word sound

continent: any one of seven large areas of land. The continents are Africa, Antarctica, Asia, Australia, Europe, North America, and South America.

culture: the way of life, ideas, and customs of a particular group of people

desert: a dry, sandy region

folktale: a story told by word of mouth from grandparent to parent to child.

Many folktales are written down in books.

Han: the name for the biggest group of Chinese people

map: a drawing or chart of all or part of Earth or the sky

martial arts: a type of exercise and a form of self-defense. Martial arts include judo, kendo, aikido, and karate.

mountain: a part of Earth's surface that rises high into the sky

plateau: a large area of high, level land

sea: a body of water that is partly enclosed by land

tradition: a custom, belief, or practice that people in a particular culture pass on to one another

TO LEARN MORE

BOOKS

Harvey, Miles. *Look What Came from China.* New York: Franklin Watts, 1998. Learn about fun foods, inventions, sports, and fashions that came all the way from China.

Jango-Cohen, Judith. *Chinese New Year.* Minneapolis: Carolrhoda Books, 2005. Read all about the Chinese New Year, a special holiday in Chinese communities.

Wang, Ping. *The Dragon Emperor.* Minneapolis: Millbrook Press, 2008. This story tells about the dragon emperor, a powerful Chinese ruler who must protect his country from a fearsome warrior named Chi You.

Young, Ed. *Lon Po Po: A Red-Riding Hood Story from China.* New York: Philomel Books, 1989. When Shang, Tao, and Paotze hear a knock at the door, they let the visitor in—but how hairy she is! Is it really their grandmother?

WEBSITES

The British Museum: Ancient China
http://www.ancientchina.co.uk/menu.html
This website from the British Museum includes information on Chinese writing, arts, crafts, history, geography, and more.

China
http://www.timeforkids.com/TFK/hh/goplaces/main/0,20344,536982,00.html
On this fun site from *Time for Kids,* you can take a virtual tour of China, learn common Chinese phrases, and send a postcard to a friend.

INDEX

The photographs in this book are used with the permission of: © China Photos/Getty Images, pp. 4, 9, 27 (bottom); © age fotostock/SuperStock, pp. 6, 8, 16, 43; © Jon Arnold Images/SuperStock, p. 7; © Bob Krist/Corbis, pp. 10, 36; © Robin Smith/Art Directors, p. 11; © Yang Liu/Corbis, p. 12; © Reed Kaestner/Corbis, p. 13; © Viviane Moos/Corbis, p. 14; © Mark Ralston/AFP/Getty Images, pp. 15, 17; © Nick & Janet Wiseman/Art Directors, p. 18; © Neil Ray/Art Directors, p. 19; © Guang Niu/Getty Images, pp. 20, 37; © Yoshio Tomii/SuperStock, p. 21; © Cory Langley, pp. 22, 26, 34; © Michael Prince/Corbis, pp. 23, 30; © Randy Faris/Corbis, p. 24; © Gareth Brown/Corbis, p. 25; © Hidekazu Nishibata/SuperStock, p. 27 (top); © Franklin Lau/Corbis, p. 28; © Bohemian Nomad Picturemakers/Corbis, p. 29; © Tibor Bognar/Art Directors, p. 31; © Asian Art & Archaeology, Inc./Corbis, p. 32; © Hu Weiming/ChinaFotoPress/Getty Images, p. 33; © FREDERIC J. BROWN/AFP/Getty Images, p. 35; © Lisette Le Bon/SuperStock, p. 38; © GOH CHAI HIN/AFP/Getty Images, p. 39; © Robert Belbin/Art Directors, p. 40; © Liu Liqun/Corbis, p. 41; © STEPHEN SHAVER/AFP/Getty Images, p. 42. Illustrations by © Bill Hauser/Independent Picture Service.

Cover: © ChinaFotoPress/ZUMA Press.